Life Amongst the Shards

Carol Victoria Di Salvo

Lulu.com
Morrisville, North Carolina

cvdinga@yahoo.com

ISBN 978-0-557-13040-5

Distributed by Lulu.com
Morrisville NC

To My family…I love you and yearn to be reunited

To My Counselor… you continue to be my buoy. Your effectiveness and sincere concern help me to work through my personal chrysalis

To My true friends…who accept me as I am…broken open

To My readers…perhaps you will find your voice in my words

Foreword

There is a story told in the Orient of a woman who went to see the wisest woman in her city for an answer to her terrifying grief over the loss of a loved one. "Why did I have to suffer this loss?" she asked. The wise woman replied, "I will help to answer your question, but first you must complete this task: go to every house in the city and get a grain of rice from every family that has never experienced loss." The grieving woman returned weeks later, empty-handed, but with a clearer vision of the enormity of the question's pervasiveness.

Grief and loss touch us all now or later, and we find ourselves grasping for answers, at times barely holding onto sanity or a sense of life's purpose. Even if the loss was years ago, a few strains of a melody, a hint of a scent, an outline of a stranger in a crowd, or just the seasonal light of the sun can bring it all back as if the months had never passed. The heart often doesn't know what year it is.

The pang of loss can be a terrorizing companion, a passage into the "valley of the shadow of death," where loneliness and uncertainty seem to reign. Yet, millions have walked that path before us, and millions are sure to follow. This experience of grief is one of the most certain events of human existence. No wonder we cry out into the darkness for something bigger than us to save us, "with rod and staff to comfort us."

If you are looking for this book of poetry to ease your grief with enchanting metaphors and hypnotically serene cadences, your search is misplaced. Carol Victoria Di Salvo has not filled these pages of her poetic diary with sweet bouquets of word-flowers meant to lull and to disarm. Instead, she has wrenched the jagged edges of shattered emotions and fractured vessels of relationships out of the depths of her grieving heart, the "shards" of a lost life. She has not striven for "nice," "pretty" or "soothing" in these poems.

What you will find here are candid, powerful, and sometimes disturbing enunciations of the depths of human grief. She may help you to find words to express out loud what your heart of sadness has at some time yearned to scream, or to comprehend in some form what another is enduring.

These poems present a diary of grief from a particular person at a selected period of her life. They show the ever-changing pitch and yaw of the storm-filled dark voyage, or the pits, brambles and uncertain footing of the moonless, desolate wandering of her soul. But don't be deluded into thinking that these writings are all about chaos and defeat. Carol Victoria Di Salvo shows us in the very enunciation of her pain that there is a kind of nobility in the railing against anguish, in the plaintiff pondering of "why did I have to suffer this loss?" She reminds us that answers only come when we push ourselves to ask the questions, and, like as not, only intense suffering seems enough to get us to dare. You will find that interspersed with her probing, sometimes searing, verses there are startling flickers of the eternal answers.

I sincerely hope that she will keep adding to this poetic diary. She shows that there truly is "life amongst the shards" for all who have ever suffered loss.

William T. Donovan

Author of *God's Powerful Plan: A Gospel of Jesus*

DEVASTATED

Sunday 14 October 2007

Images are frozen, forever seared vividly in my mind.

The worst **HAS** happened. There is nothing else to fear.

Injustice once again

WHY? Don't even try to answer that because there is **NO ACCEPTABLE** answer!

I am in **HELL!**

I am free falling and the **"SPLAT"** can't come quick enough.

People talk about "still being connected"...Yeah?
I want to feel that **NOW**!

Black isn't a dark enough color for how my spirit feels.

I hate the question: "How are you doing?"
Who wants the real answer?
Can **anyone** handle the real answer?

THE PIT

Thursday 18 October 2007

For awhile your life is spent on the rim
With glimpses of the pit
But never really grasping the magnitude of the depth

Until...
That first freefall in....is like nothing you can relate to....
Alien is too familiar a word, because you've seen movies.....
But the **PIT?**

No one is **EVER** ready for being summoned to the **PIT.**
And yeah, there are those who tell of "surviving the **PIT"....**But no one really does.

How can you?

Your sentence **IS LIFE!**

ALONE IN A CROWD

Saturday 20 October 2007

When time was innocent and unscathed, I didn't understand.

Oh, to still not understand....if only.

But now

Loneliness in a crowd is suffocating and claustrophobic.

You become invisible while you are being trampled by shoes whose soles you are untouched by.

That is when you realize the true definition of

A - L - O - N - E

ARE YOU THERE?

Monday 22 October 2007

To be insignificant in another person's life is to not exist.
If I don't
To whom does it matter?

It used to matter...
Not now.

Who would know?
To find out...I'm gone...would be an inconvenience, nothing more.

THE CLUB OF SCARS

Thursday 25 October 2007

Some organizations have ritual handshakes in order to recognize and admit members.

The requirements are minimal and painless and willingly accepted by those wishing to join.

Jackets are proudly worn and meetings eagerly attended.

The Club of Scars on the other hand, needs no announced recruitment drive.

Like a heat-seeking missile, life time members are initiated.

The choice of when, is a haphazard circumstance and grappling with non-membership is unheard of, their pleas falling on deaf ears.

No matter how much a potential member runs trying in vain to escape the claws of recruitment the strangling hold are all consuming.

Yet....it is virtually unrecognizable who is a member.

There are no jackets or meetings, no ritual handshakes and there isn't a stadium huge enough to hold a convention because **EVERYONE** who has a pulse is a **SCAR** in the making and membership is **NOT OPTIONAL!**

DO YOU HEAR IT?

Friday 26 October 2007

The silence is deafening.
How can the quiet be s o o o O O O loud?
I turn on the radio and still it's blaring.

Wherever I roam, the blare follows me.
It's as if the volume control button is stuck on MAXIMUM!

Can you go deaf from the pitch of silence?
Or just lose your mind?

Either would be a relief.

THE VIEW

Sunday 4 November 2007

What was will never be.

And now, at times, I wonder...if it is still?

It **has** to be!

An observer, visions the status quo.

Yet from the realistic myopic lens, life is a wilderness that is deep, dark and dank.

You are chaffing from the turbulence of standing still and the blindfold is fused into your skin.

Your inner fuse is spark-deprived from restlessness.

The human spirit has its own pyre that with each personal loss you enter and feel the scorch of the flames and smell the essence of your soul joining your remembered loved one.

LEFT BEHIND

Tuesday 13 November 2007

In this barren existence, in an otherwise crowded world,
I am lost and wandering aimlessly.

The familiar is no longer.
I have **lost** my umbilical connection.

Life is displaced and I am a refugee in a world of sojourners...
Longing for home and loved ones whose DNA is mine.

BLOCKING

Thanksgiving Day 22 November 2007

Consciously making today an UN-DAY
A deletion on my calendar
Pulling down the shades on the panes of glass of my soul
Seeking hibernation in slumber to bring a night to this unwanted day
Turning a deaf ear to the scratching of nails on the chalkboard greetings of well wishers
Why don't they know it's been **CANCELLED!**
The honored guests are unavailable...and no one has an appetite.

It is not what memories recall.
It is not what my soul hungers...
And how great both of these are.

In the past, it was not cherished, as it is now, if it was to be again, even for a fleeting moment.
The guest without family was perplexing to my pristine vision.
But yet...their "UNDAY" of the past...is present to me today,
As *I am* seated in *their* chair at today's table.

ABANDONED

Monday 26 November 2007

I am left behind.
Not by choice....but by sentencing.

The aftermath from the emotional fallout...
The nuclear disaster of my soul
Scrambling for some reason or will to go forward

The pier is empty.
The vessel has left.
It is cold and raw...and I can't get warm.
My cord has been severed...and I am frozen on the edge.

A FINE LINE

Thursday 29 November 2007

Have you vanished? **POOF....**and you're gone?
Have I been abducted?
Have I lost my mind?

Or....is everything that was no more than a dream that I have now awakened from?

Am I seeing the future or the past....because the present is all interference on the picture screen?

Was life as I remember and yearn for never a reality?
If so...**HOW** can I enter into that realm while awake?
Or be in a constant dream in order to live?

Without either, I am a zombie in a land of aliens.

THE TSUNAMI

Friday 7 December 2007

All along the prediction was tentative...a delicately thin pane of glass.

Caressed and nurtured with immeasurable concern.

In hoping for the best and wanting to believe,

I was thought to be in denial or unaware of reality.

And even though I didn't get an OSCAR....my acting "as if"... must have been that good because fear was always my secret companion.

Trying to "live in the moment" may have looked believable...

I fooled them...but never myself.

It was the forecasters who took us by surprise...

It was as if they were speaking another language

Or I was suddenly a foreigner displaced and unable to comprehend...

THIS CAN'T BE HAPPENING!

And....as we ran for her life...to outrun the encroaching TSUNAMI... we were stumbling and grappling to regain some ground...

When all along we were in quick sand and sinking rapidly...being swallowed - up....as if our hands were tied as the **grim reaper** approached.

With our eyes w i d e o p e n and the lights glaring, we witnessed

The TSUNAMI OF OUR HEARTS

The aftermath of which....no one survived...

No matter what the monitor records

THE SILENCING

Sunday 6 December 2007

I feel like I've lost my voice...
The conversation is taking place, but I can't speak the words.
There is a gag tightly secured that no hands can undo.
It is the silencing of conversations that is pushing me to the brink.
I don't think I can thrive let alone survive the sentence I've been given.

The thought of going on is impossible and suffocating.
The race I need to endure leaves me breathless and in a panic.

In the quiet of my thoughts
In the darkness of the night
The internal turmoil erupts like a volcano spewing the lava of my soul.

THE CAIRN

Monday 31 December 2007

The foundation...is the LIFE to our years shared

Of our hands joined
And our hearts one

Of our laughter being unstoppable
And our tears being dried by one another

Of our understanding and knowing
When we were distraught

Of our holding-up
While falling down

Of our "**believing"**
When there was no reason to...other than faith in each other

And as fragile as the cairn viewed by a stranger may seem...
Its strength is in the LIFE our years shared!

ACID TEARS

Sunday 13 January 2008

The wretchedness of pain **swells up** and you are overcome with acid tears burning down your face...as you place each foot that weighs a ton on the dark pavement that lies ahead in the night.

Where you are going....doesn't matter...as your grief is your steady companion.

Wanting to just collapse where you are...seems compelling...

But you would never get up...so fear and uncertainty keep you moving

You know this monsoon of acid tears will return...

But its arrival does like a thief in the night...

Know not the hour, but certain it will.

I AM

Monday 21 January 2008

In ANGUISH...I turn to you
In DESPAIR...I call out your name
In DESPARATION...I hope I am heard
In LONELINESS...I seek your company
In FEAR...I give you my concerns
In LETHARGY...you are my energy and inspiration
In MY DARKNESS...I need your presence
In SLEEP...I wish for a visit
In MY SALTY TEARS...I taste your love
In THE QUIET...I listen for your voice
In NOT SEEING...I yearn for you
In BEAUTY...I remember your appreciation and respect of nature
In LAUGHTER...I recall times spent with you doing so
In WAITING...I need endurance until we are reunited.

UNTIL

Monday 4 February 2008

Until...you have been tempered in the scorching fire of loss and felt the searing blisters of your soul...you...do not understand the pain.

Until...all those that you have been lovingly nourished by are gone...you...do not understand the hunger.

Until...your world...as you knew it, is obliterated from your familiar tread...you...do not understand the barrenness of the days to come.

Until...your *shared memories* are *only stories* to someone...you...do not understand the tie that binds that has been severed.

Until...

Then...*you may* have a *glimpse* of the uncertain journey I am on.

A DECISION

Saturday 9 February 2008

In the stillness of a dawn
Holding the mysteries yet to be revealed
Your nocturnal desperate hours must have seemed endless.

You find yourself at Life's Cross Road.
One path seems the way to go...Yet...
You realize there may still be a truer way...that in the splitting of a hair you reach for.

You said..."It was the hardest thing you ever did."

And you gave me the rope attached to your anchor.
And together we witnessed the road still to be traveled.

ON THE JOURNEY

Wednesday 19 March 2008

Will my thirst ever be quenched?
My hunger ever satiated?
My fatigue ever energized?
My eye sight ever 20/20?
My strained expression ever relaxed?
My uncertain directions ever find a compass?

Will you be my ever companion?
Helping as you always did.
Making the load lighter and the darkness light

My shoes, as I, are worn and scuffed.

But...when I get a sense of your essence...
I AM!!!

EXILE

Saturday 10 May, 2008

To be emotionally severed from those who gave your life roots… is to wither on the vine

As all nourishment is unattainable

To be insignificant… as though you are transparent

And the view beyond is the one that is valued

To realize…. it is up to you, whatever you do…

Is not freedom but prison without a parole

To be a puzzle piece that will always be odd…

As the solution, in the joining is no longer on the board

To be in exile… with a compass that can't spin to true N…

Is another direction leading to HELL!

PLAYING A ROLE

Saturday 14 June 2008

The fibers of the threads are like tentacles wrapping around my body...
As I slip my arms into the sleeves of the required uniform

I don't fit into this body cast...I never did...but more so now
That was then...

"May I help you?"
To whom am I offering help?
You or myself...as we both are wounded

Perhaps, during the transaction, we are both the customer in this moment of life; each paying a price...one with currency and the other with self.

I don't have the resources.
Perhaps, you have something to give?

LIFE AMONGST THE SHARDS

Friday 27 June 2008

I feel like Humpty Dumpty...

Fragmented...

The pieces of my soul don't fit back together

Nor is there glue with enough holding power to make me whole again

I didn't know my life was that close to the edge...

Until that fateful fall into my bottomless abyss that has become my day to day reality

The breaking of the spirit can never be reset, as the fault line is invisible to the naked eye

Until...the next quake and the spewing of emotions that seemed manageable are now more insipid... as they've had time to marinate their own flavor and texture in what life is becoming.

NORMAL

Saturday 19 July 2008

Nothing will ever be as it was

Overwhelming loss

Rage at life's unfairness

Memories precious and bittersweet

Always a part of who we are

Love that is everlasting

But "normal"?

....never again...

LET ME IN

Friday 17 October 2008

Am I holding you back from your journey?
The one I don't have a ticket for...at least not yet
If so, it may be selfish, but I hunger to tag along, even slightly

Remember me tagging along in another life and time?

That was only yesterday....

Now, in the many rooms....emptiness awaits and time and place are meaningless.

If I knock, will you answer?

DESOLATION

Monday 26 January 2009

Desolation is a weight I can't put down

I reach for the elixir….to numb and suspend

I am tired of superficial; the mask is tattered from the friction of life

I hunger for the genuine which, when revealed I see a frozen reflection from fellow pilgrims

As avoidance is their mantra

It is too much work to go on!

Being is energy-sapping enough!

Life is a treadmill….that reaps exhaustion.

EXIT Stage 4

Sunday 12 July 2009

Everyone is given an exit script

When yours arrives or how long your role last is out of your control

The drama that unfolds is played without an understudy off in the wings

The role, as you, is an original that only you get to play out

The die is cast

When the final curtain comes down, there are no curtain calls
As you have already been summoned to your lifetime role
And the theatre is dark and empty

THY WILL BE DONE

Saturday 29 August 2009

Thy will be done
As we are given a diagnosis that forever changed our lives
And receive the courage to face the days to follow

Thy will be done
As we collapse and are carried when our world implodes
For we are sapped and void of strength to get up ourselves

Thy will be done
As we don't see any reason to go on
As we yet wander on Emmaus Road searching and lost

Thy will be done
As we weather our storm
And fellow pilgrims are brought into our lives
Offering to have us flow on their tailwind as our wings are broken

Thy will be done
Until the veil of this life is parted
And we pass through to our new birth

Thy will be done

About the Author

Carol Victoria Di Salvo is a resident of Long Island, New York. She continues to write poetry and personal reflections, while devoting time to restoring her childhood home.

www.ingramcontent.com/pod-product-compliance
Ingram Content Group UK Ltd.
Pitfield, Milton Keynes, MK11 3LW, UK
UKHW041840200726
13854UKWH00003BA/1230